The Story They Told Us of Light

for Virginia
and for James Seay

The Story They Told Us of Light

POEMS

BY RODNEY JONES

THE UNIVERSITY OF
ALABAMA PRESS
TUSCALOOSA

The University of Alabama Press
Tuscaloosa, Alabama 35487-0380
uapress.ua.edu

Typeface: Caledonia

Manufactured in the United States of America
Cover design: Anna F. Jacobs

∞
The paper on which this book is printed meets the minimum requirements of American National Standard for Information Science–Permanence of Paper for Printed Library Materials, ANSI Z39.48-1984.

Paperback ISBN: 978-0-8173-0035-7

A previous edition of this book has been catalogued by the Library of Congress as follows:

Library of Congress Cataloging in Publication Data

Jones, Rodney, 1950–
The story they told us of light.

I. Title
PS3560.05263S8 811'.5'4 79-20954
ISBN 0-8173-0029-5 (cloth)
ISBN 0-8173-0035-X (paper)

ACKNOWLEDGMENTS

I thank the Tennessee Arts Commission for a grant that allowed me to finish several poems in this volume, and I thank the editors of the following journals, in which some of the poems in this book were first published. Grateful acknowledgment to the following:

Barataria #3: "Loose Ends" and "Opinions of Day and Night." Copyright © 1977 by Barataria.

The Black Warrior Review: "A Cure For Shapes," "Honor," "Looking Natural," "O Wordsworth," and "The Whittler Hums Amazing Grace." Copyright © 1975, 1976, 1979 by The Black Warrior Review.

The Greensboro Review #12: "For My Friend Shot Six Times By An Irate Husband." Copyright © 1972 by the University of North Carolina at Greensboro.

Intro IV: "Micro Journey," which was originally published in a slightly different form as "Micro Journey From The House of Religion." Copyright © 1971 by Bantam Books.

Puddingstone #6: "The Abandoned Fairgrounds at Austinville." Copyright © 1977 by Puddingstone.

Shenandoah, Fall 1970: "Extensions of Watts Bar Dam," which was first published in a slightly different form as "Watts Bar Dam," in volume 22, number 1. Copyright © 1970 by Washington and Lee University, reprinted from *Shenandoah:* The Washington and Lee University Review with the permission of the Editor.

Southern Poetry Review, Winter 1975: "Crushed Objects At The Bottom of a Still Pool." Copyright © 1975 by Southern Poetry Review.

The Small Farm: "After The Sermon," which originally appeared in a slightly different form as "Measurements of Gravity," "American Forest," "Bean Station, Late Twenties: A Letter to Fred Chappell," "Chainsaw," "David Druid Richard Alexander Jones," "Dulcimer," "For Asphalt For Concrete For Keeping Things Solid," "Going Ahead, Looking Back," "Homebreaking," "On Leaving the Farm," "The Story They Told Us of Light," and "Undercover." Copyright © 1977, 1978 by The Small Farm.

Vanderbilt Poetry Review: "Driving in Floodwater." Copyright © 1977 by Vanderbilt Poetry Review.

"Debris" and "Extensions of Watts Bar Dam" appeared in *White Trash*, New South Company, 1977.

Several of the poems in this volume appeared in *Going Ahead, Looking Back,* a limited edition published by Southbound Books, 1978.

CONTENTS

The Story They Told Us of Light

I

FOR ASPHALT FOR CONCRETE FOR KEEPING THINGS SOLID

First, I'll unpin my wings,
let them float up over the riverside
like prayers. May
their disappearance be substantial.

Next, I'll take the earth
as proposition: its aromas
intrigue me, its southerly winds
satellite to breath.

I won't have to say the lives
of the animals, those squirrels
who have made up their minds,
tagged deer clicking in the mist.

Only I'll follow the cold
until it hardens, and when it surfaces
in debt or a woman's eyes
I'll acknowledge its remarkable alloys.

For a few hard seconds, I'll give
away hours, a few doomed bugs,
a few twitches along the gray
involuntary muscle of the sidewalk.

It won't mean much to the asphalt.
It won't say much to the concrete.
Both duct and paved lot will hum
to the slow cello in the root.

And you will want to repeat the notes—
flare, soften, then crumble—
to know them as a deaf man knows
that no one is playing a saxophone.

It's not important, even as I spoke,
I could feel the oil rising,
the old traffic in my head
beginning to slip out into the purlieus.

HOMEBREAKING

This morning I was sure
the sun had not shone before
the maple leaves fired
so high, the jimsonweed
had never stood so slender
and dew came for the first time
to resilver the old mailbox
to spot the apples with rust
so I took the finest, the ripest
the firmest of all apples
into my hands and it was
the world reduced to pleasure
raised it to my lips as though
breast had never needed body
to be lovely or live, ah
and mouth, savoring that expected
sweetness, opened fully
and I spat out first hollowness
then yellowjackets, then poems.

ON LEAVING THE FARM

The land does not need us like we need the land,
the same figure, grounds for marriage or divorce:
the first time I lost it I was ten, day
dreaming sad Pip in that England over the horizon
while our B-Farmhall spun and bucked to light
on its side in a ditch, its tires treading air.
Twelve springs in the saddle, I could not plough
the furrow straight, but jolted in the wrong gear,
leveling fences and hedgerows like a red conspiracy,
grew muscles like a fish, but cursed hay bales into barns.
When I left, some ancient tension in the fields
must have relaxed its hold, the sun's breath
turned into grass and cattle grazed the lost rows.
Faraway, my family, all farmers, spin in their bones.

KANSAS

There we were in jail with no money but no expenses,
Unsleeping at the last turn of guard, mad for solace,
Saddled in hard cots, wondering what tattooed hands
Had grimed the cards. Were they the same as those
That scribbled love and arrowed assholes on the walls?
Here was another American hostel of the blues,
Keeping the only truly dark secrets while dispensing
The outrage, as Kansas might loan New York
Her only souls worth keeping. Outside on the prairie
The wind was shooting snowy shrapnel against the houses.
We could see that much in the streetlights and real
People who like Kansas were dry and distant.

for John Allison

Many roads go to the crest
of a hill and turn into maple trees,
a drop into water boiling rock
or a pasture where the barn
that seemed for a moment to be
a ship half sunk in honeysuckle
is grabbed by headlights and shaken.
On every road but the right one
hay abandoned for thirty years
is falling into your eyes,
the hurt smile of your windshield
gradually losing its teeth, while
the radio, softer by the hour, repeats
the latest songs, and you wait
for hunters to come in from the cold.

And so we touch ourselves awake,
or stop for coffee. The waitress,
her hair blonde and highly technical,
might be had for twenty dollars,
or loneliness. You don't know. You
feed two quarters to the jukebox—
it whirs another galaxy, a million years,
then plays what might have been,
in bed, or on the road.
A blizzard, two states away, working
through the soft eyes of herefords,
moving into the cabs of diesels
moving south: you hear it as you pay,
snowdrifts in the voices
of friendly truckers wincing at the bar.

But mostly it's houses along the way,
the young wife of the farmer
lying awake in the dark, thinking of you
as you were ten years ago,
taking her from the farm, her life
that is going nowhere—as you think
of her, delicious, slender as a wand—
both of you wrong and right
the instant your shadow turns her wall
that color between green and grey.
Graves should be opener than
some houses, communities that send
you, failsafe, into thin, spleenless air.
You want your lock picked
and your door broken before it rots.

The road does that, the road grows old.
You know you've been asleep
for miles, your heart horsing the wheel
like a lunker out of the bushes.
How much farther between the eyes
you slap yourself back, remembering
someone shouting no way to get there
from here? No truth but in things?
You sing until there's gravity
in your throat, and the stars click
out of their places, letting the day
fall gently across the hog lots
and across the little creeks you begin
to recognize, lighting a room
where your place is set at the table.

GROUND RULES

The yard is no longer
than a nonswimmer might
maneuvre to safety,
no wider than a bulb shows.
A child with a toy shovel
measures its bottom,
the bent finger of an old man
points higher than it goes.
Columbine, thrush and chickweed
mark its borders
and hickories compose on air
the words of its constitution.
To be mistaken for a citizen
one has only to sit down
and breathe deeply enough
to support "Hello."
One votes for weather,
the lethargy of rugs
or exhaustion of turtles.
As in a prison, the way out
is by thought, a ride
on a train whistle or song,
a town where one marries
the first presentable woman,
the daughter of someone big,
and fathers a son, Tony.
Then the rest of life
there's shade in August,
firewood by January.
Then a man is no different
from bush, leaf or grass.
Then it is the same
effort, waking or sleeping.
To leave is to return.
To stay is to be moved.

STARLINGS

Not an individualist among them,
no sleek ambassador, no Geronimo,
neither queen nor cock of the walk,
but suddenly they are here, alight
on the mossed branches of the pecan
as though wrung from a soiled cloud
heaped in the laundry bin of heaven—
here as when in my thirteenth October
I raised my shotgun to their flock,
and stumbling mid-air, collapsed
like stringless plumb bobs, or spinning
in a soft, improbable snowfall,
they hammered the muck of my father's field.
Do I only imagine their gift for rebirth?
A catch in air, a flutter, and they begin
to move across the bruised terraces
drawn by the maps in their wings
pausing by ponds and barn lots
to peck at the secret corn in pig dung
and then rise in a scaffolding of heart
beat and wing beat, to settle again
like bleak blossoms in the single tree
of my childhood, turning each limb
into an abacus of shrieking consonants,
filibustering their windy politic
for all bad singers and wearers of black.
Brothers, unloved or damned
for a bum talent or ugliness,
I have no idea how the dead rise
in the minds of the living,
bearing out of the forgotten details
the language of tin and unoiled bearings,
or why today when I heard that song
I wanted less to live. And so
came to sing in a kind of prayer
no god would want to hear
of what it is to rise and what it is to fall,
inventing mercy.

THE BATHROOM DREAM OF THE ADOLESCENT

Seeing mother naked, like the first view
of an island, her breasts lofted from the white bath:
a great deal of splashing: the walls are glass
and only this one room has been dreamed.
The door opens only in, the mirror is steamed.
So what can you do at 12? No place to play
a record, no elsewheres but this one.

You see her eyes for once warm and foreign,
a language you can't comprehend and one pink toe
beckoning all the waters of your body to sprout hair,
to surface. Even if you do sleep fitfully
once you admiralled a plastic dish in the commode.
When you touch flesh, the walls shatter.
Awake, you think you've dreamed of daddy.

FOR WOMEN WITH BLUE HAIR

Not words, but the ghosts of condolences,
the well-meaning dried arrangements
dripping their last rust
colored berries into the music box
as it tinks away, *Scheherazade*.

Hour on hour, as you read
that lovely girl, Jane Austen,
the wind tried the makework of the gardeners,
a pelting in the phlox, and peonies
sent their white notes to earth.

In your warm house
you could not get warm enough
but kept moving to other rooms,
wan, perturbed,
as if the kidneys were a lover.

I think now it must be time
you put the ointment on,
and swallow the bitter pills
that will sustain your heart
until morning.

Then leave this poem
for your own, the one we know
so well, which begins
with cats, sweet rose and moon,
the old flames that burn around you.

LOOKING NATURAL

The day is tethered to a fine mist, and
the sky—the sky does not exist. There

is, on channel 48, an educated bloodworm,
a cat catwalking a gangplank of air, and

now, moon-eyed, he drifts into his funny, whacked-
out shape on the sidewalk, and

the dogs—the dogs go about their business
of resembling trustees of multi-national

conglomerates, and the telephone opens
a crack in the morning. And from

this instance I must drive to the Peck
Funeral Home, and grief is numb and precise.

In death, my grandmother's face is
close-lipped and sullen, and there is

something of the mannequin in her sewn-
in mouth, in the powdered hollows of

her cheeks and the drawn smoothness under her
eyes, and all around her, the obtuse,

obese friends are gesturing like nymphs
escaped from some civic ballet, and

removed to the corridor, the men are talking
of cropdusting and Harry Truman, and the

elderly visitors from Summerford Rest Home
creak and totter like pulleys in rotting

wellhouses, and they greet me with glossy
photos of pink children in blue play-

suits with tiny golden bears embroidered on
the collars, and I nod to them and smile,

passing out into the mild afternoon
turning blue with such a compelling sadness.

In one tongue, *Heaven*.
In another, *Hawaii*.

Both islands, green-aged, so far
from the little minister
who would gather all the meaning
in one terrible fist
then slam it into the pulpit
as though a fire had started.
All loftiness suspended, dinners
his leviathan blessing rendered
the rawest bird palatable;
he had the politician's gift,
local everywhere he went.

That summer record numbers
were altered to mothering waters.
The sanctuary aisle tilted
like the deck of a sinking ship.
June will never find such days,
how they rotted into the dark
fabric of our smallest talk:
sunlight articulating the divide
where grass met sky,
the unmodulated syllables
of the funeral director
the night my grandmother died.
For any voice too large
to narrow to coherence, my sister
embroidered her quaint expletive
on silence: "stars, my stars."

What is the word for that time
and the mountain range
between now and then, that piano
too old to hold a tune,
full of hands, corroded strings
and the elephant, pitched
just far enough from harmony
to fit the human voice?

The old woman played softly—
I learned to sing each song
the way it was written: by heart,
the last verse first,
the refrain faint to mean more,
as if to cock the ears of daylilies.

Who could tell from this distance
which of us in the choir
were only opening and shutting
our mouths, but artfully?

Once I penciled the word hyacinth
on a clean sheet of paper,
sounding it again and again;
finally, it was no more
than the wind recites
with the billion tongues
of the maple tree—"to wish, to wish."

Now of that time I would translate
there is a holding space
beyond the clock's semantics
and a few famous for breathlessness
entered in the etymology of dust,
a method or lesson in the leaving:
how each thing has its language,
if only we knew how to read it.

ADAM'S APPLE

The important food is not swallowed.
It bobs like an anchor under the tongue.
In an hour of silent prayer
the neck is as expressive as the face,
almost transparent, rolling its oiled bearing.
Except for that, you were perfect!
Others managed good to kneel,
                                        you floated
and over the solemn breathing of the organ,
the candles arching to the new year,
the worshipers could hear
the rise and fall of your breasts.
Among those simple hearts, those pedestrians
of the spirit, you danced under eyelids
and testified without speaking.
Neither was it necessary to speak.
Prayer was a kind of listening, if for you.
Some words I tried to eat, then
their euphemisms, finally even the roots
proved too heavy. But how shyly
you bowed your head. You knew
why dogs and kisses went for the throat.

GOITER

A woman with a potato on her neck,
powdered and enraptured like a spaniel,
is listening for the golden harp
in Reverend Otto Winton's voice.
Far from the sea, the piano softens
for remembering, and I remember.

Where the lame and disfigured came
to be healed, there was a sermon
straight from palsy to the deathbed.
There was a spot above the tonsils
tender as the skin under the thumbnail.
Touched there, who would not weep?

Often the deacons appeared to sleep
and the homely swiveled like owls
to prey on tall boys whose squirming
fit the preacher's exact description
of desperate men shaken by conviction.
The right way to look was serene,

prim and single-minded as monuments.
To look there is to be looked-at.
But who will look the right way now
out of such a past? If I remember:
the last prayer was to be made whole;
the first was to be beautiful.

II

THE STORY THEY TOLD US OF LIGHT

There was a plan to save everyone—
Nights of the last century, dim lights
From each hamlet and mill town—
By every lamp, a woman and a bible—

The men with storm lanterns, wading
In backgrowth, divided on trails—
Scent of the coon, scent of the fox,
Moon song of red bone and blue tick—

But the stars, as always, cold, barbed—
The heifer lowing in her new heat—
When the doors were closed a last time—
After breath turned the rooms dark

And the wicks slumped in their tin bowls—
That other motion, of the mind,
Which made light of the wind
And saw at windows the white eye of the beast.

DULCIMER

Out of chicory spliced in hedgerow,
Out of ramp and bitterroot, polk
And wood sorrel, from the old house
With two rooms spreading newspapers
Against the cold, from bear tracks
In the lot, through the paralyzed light

Of barns coiled in privet, from spring
To river, firing white, rocking
For lowlands, your life comes,
Wherever it meant, becoming, to go,
To one string ringing over the body
Of a sleeping woman, her ribs

Stained from chestnut and sassafras,
The dark heart hollowed there,
And two strings asleep in the moon's
Icy briars, dripping on clematis
And stone, and the valley sleeping
Beside the mountain, its peaks

Great snow patches of bluet
And cinquefoil, balsam and rhododendron,
The farmer sleeping by the seamstress,
Two strings asleep, the other dreaming
In the perfect pitch of gospels, how
You heard the diamondback once, and knew.

DAVID DRUID RICHARD ALEXANDER JONES, *1819–1858*

All March it was winter, drizzle
And typhoid plucked two daughters
So that in April he gave to his slaves
Themselves, left seed unplanted

And rode a stallion into the laurels
Into a blue sheath of the Cumberland Mountains
To drink all day alone. Whatever
In that shade he found stays secret

Whether by drink he plumbed the trees'
Consciousness, or by prayer wrung
Warm rain from recondite clouds:
By July his liver shrank to a cobweb.

Then a neighbor woman brought a young hen
To the widow, and chrysanthemums
Stood in a clear bowl by the window.
A nervous tenor sang the body into earth.

Our names outlive us. The body recedes
And the soul forgets, the soul whirls
Out of the mouth of a flower, the body
Catches on a root, white, and disappears.

The name rides high like a pennant
That flares and shudders long after the parade
Has marched by and no one can remember
Any reason for the music or the dancing.

Of my grandfather's grandfather
I keep five words, five words chiseled on a slate shim
That sinks in humus
By a path grown over with cowvines—

That, and a story, the knowledge that what passes
From fathers to sons—a sallowness
Along the cheekbones, a corkscrew in the ankle
Meaning rain, or story—winnows

Until there are no names but root and seed,
The laurel turned new by sunlight
And something in soil that will not give up,
Something as hard as a button on a coat.

DRIVING IN FLOODWATER

Past the last fenceposts,
bearded sedge,
riffles in the tops of willows,
there is a moment

when all that I remember
is wrong for this place
lit by two moons
and the twin beams of my headlights,

flotillas as though dreamed,
leaf mould and milk jug,
drowned birdnests
of fur and cramped bone,

and further,
where yesterday the corn shoots
ascended in green nipples,
I listen for the gravel

to tell if I'm in the rut
or out of line, try to judge
from the surface
if the whirlpool's clot and sneer

means the bridge is gone
or holds, drive slowly,
turn and the planks rumble
under my wheels, drive slowly,

turn and the road rises
from water like a hand,
but my own hand,
which is shaking, knows

as it feels for the pocket
what the eye cannot see,
that we reach out for nothing,
touching a coin or a key.

UNDERCOVER

One hair divides the light,
Eye returns it like a ball
But dark is unanimous
Where the millwright's son
Clenches his eyelids till
A peacock flares its tail,
Orange, blue and green feathers
Comforting as a glass
Of milk or funk of socks
Hidden under the pillow
When the laser cuts through
To sleep and the whippoorwill
Calls three times from
The rot in the broken comb
Of the treetop and he is sure
Three cracks have opened
In the magenta face of God,
But it is nothing of course
It is nothing but a bur
That has worked its way under
The feathers, and that is why
The whippoorwill moans so
Disconsolately and the wind
Pushes the branches of the pecan
Tree against the windowscreen
And there is no comfort in knowing
That no one has ever seen a ghost.

THE ABANDONED FAIRGROUNDS AT AUSTINVILLE

To the horse, the world is clear pasture
where three Hungarians dismantled the stage:
grass our only ghost town, green wires
from vaudeville. For years, perhaps one
starling has been knitting an endless worm
from the droppings. Calves stand half attentive
like the salute of a hungry corporal
with a fly in his eyebrow. On clear days
the pattern begins in mountain. No one holds
his girl without the thought: *marry me
in this theatre.* Out here, the only caretakers
are blind. The great birds pass without opinions.
By night light, you might have seen
the last burlesque show, the horses vacuumed
past wombs, the lives of the farmers who watched
or thought they saw a woman swallow buffalo
nickels with her private parts. If there's a
ticket left, it's framed and sold at auction.
Lovers rise from the grass, insects drone in the hollow—
wind off a rain, the wind from up valley.
The horse sleeps, or it is that quiet.

ABSENCE OF AFFECTION

When they first plunge out into the light,
the horses, I mean, their manes held aloft

as if by some disembodied electricity
in the wind, you think it's their desire

driving hooves into the soft muck forward
but they stop like you do, at the fence:

below on the freeway, a watermelon truck
passes a Volkswagen. If there's a spy

smoking along in his Volvo, you can bet
he's on his way to a barber or masturbating

to stay awake. Like phantoms or strangers,
each predilection threatens then dissolves

into a loneliness not attached to your own.
Admit it. Weren't you expecting majesty

when you first followed the horses,
and they're still out there, at the fence:

below, morticians and vegetarians are
passing, each promise lifted, like the moment

following the best lay of your life
when you remember she did not say she loved you.

CHAIN SAW

Begin with a thicket. You will work
Your way up to forests, the swells
Of foothills, softwood to deciduous
Gold, beech to sycamore, past the oaks
To balsam and spruce, walking
The balds, then down again through maples,
Ash and poplar, down through cedar,
Herding pines to the river
On the mad amplified droning of bees,
But hearing always behind you, the music
Behind the doors, the new rooms
Where women in yellow nightgowns
Are snapping off their lamps, the tables
Abandoned now, the dishes in cabinets,
Only that distant breathing and laughter
As timbers slow-motion to crush their shadows
And you know, if only for awhile,
There is grace on the earth.

AMERICAN FOREST

Backside of nowhere, Alabama,
green sails of loblollies climb
out of ruts settlers made
going back home. Dying, my
grandfather showed me terraces
under tall trees, limestone
washed up like drowned sheep,
bushes wild haired as prophets
where well-behaved crops had grown.
Trees he knew as well as settlers
who hung their names on coves
repossessed by glum storekeepers.
Those orphans of the forest
went ahead of us and behind us,
and for awhile, our lives were
those trees stopping at a clearing,
fenceposts split and greyed by snow,
the latticework of a well house
scrawled in hieroglyphs of kudzu,
and those two elderly lovers,
the chimneys, remembering the ashes
like a nightgown at their feet.
At a stump, we paused, considering
shade, then started back down
the mountain, guns on our shoulders.
Our steps made the deer invisible.

For awhile, each voice shares an edge
you think common: women become figurines
to be held, fingered and talked to sex.
At each door, words, as if to prove you breathe,
are required, and when you enter, each glass
is filled by your word. But one night you come
to a thicket you thought was clearing

and think you know how the anthropologist
must have felt, staring through the empty sockets
of the skull of some pre-sapient hominid.
Surely it was this darkness driving him,
the moist breath of cuddly animals turned predator.
And you reach deep past your throat for words
and one comes out: the talisman, the misunderstood.

Every house drinks from the same lake,
A white spool of water paying wire,
And there is a taste for other fires:
A desperation in locked cylinders
And a pale amber that darkens the glass.
There are doors closing behind doors
And windows fastened over windows.
Once you pointed to a tree, then the lights
Went out, but we could see in the mind's eye
Down the thickening, iced-over branches
Of highways, over the hidden branches
Of water and light, the sap stalled
At the center: a semi tortoise-backed
In the grass beside the snapped pole
Dangling its broken connections. You
Put down your glass. "South of Louisville
An inch of snow would cripple God."
Now, I examine the television
As a doctor would his wealthiest patient—
There, where everyone is thief or comedian
And no one has long to live. The tree
Though, still waits to be explained,
And its branches go every way they can.
The air admits them without notable pain.
It recovers clarity for each fallen leaf.
It is our minds that make us unlike that.
Though our nerves are roots and systems
Gathering life to coldest consideration,
And the city extends to us the outermost tips
Of its branches, we are not the trees.
We are blunter than that, softer,
We can go by eye where the sun prints
Lichens on trunk-colored stone,
And like the trunk, the stone is full
Of our misunderstanding. As the tree
Holds summer in its trunk, I draw into myself
A life that was public—leaves, blossoms—
If only to reach for you inside these trees,
Inside these shells of trees, to say,
With so few odors, you can smell the moon.

O WORDSWORTH

I went for a lonely walk
in the cacophony, woods vernal
to the hilt, flush with
Aprilish bees mad for last light
and might have walked farther
into darkness but sat down
on a dumb log beside a white
party of fungi. Heard
the wind blow laurel, thrush
and ant word, the sky
oysterish. All the way to
the river, I could hear
the shrill, hatched assassins.

MICRO JOURNEY

It is like walking
On the skin of a banjo
Walking with you
This early in the green season.
I can hear our steps

In the pinpoint eardrums
Of tiny insects
Who clutch each other
In a world of tall wires.
Complexity envelops them

And seeing everything
A thousand ways
Drives the green blood
To a frenzy. But
They have their own faith

And their own genius.
Consider the bee.
Think of living in a house
The size of a sundial.
No room for

Extra furniture: a love
Commode, if you insist,
But nothing extraordinary.
The road we took in
Has been lost and is

Grass, grassed over twice.
By our movement of feet
Let each small other also
Move, away from thresholds
Trying to get inside.

DEBRIS

At last, the pillows would take our heads
Which have held all day the thoughts of nothing
In particular, only we have wanted
So much of girls and grace, an understanding
With the wind, a kinship with white houses.

And all evening, it has seemed there have been
Too many words, but none specific enough.
The convoy passed, containing young reserves,
The jokes they told escaped us
While rain unsnapped samaras from the elm.

It was a day of wobbly passes thrown at our feet,
Of softballs yellowing just beyond
Our outstretched gloves, and we would release
Those hours at once, like tickets or tamed birds,
We would lie down without voices, without nerves.

But for some time, our oaths have softened
Against the plaster; the lights thinning out
For miles, and echoes returning, old, diminished,
Their aspirates scuffed on sand rock
Or hung in the moist branches of the hydrangea.

Until it seems all this year has been
A dim window and snoring from another room.
Debris of my days, untouchables, I think the moon
Sent down your code, but I could not read it.
I give this calling to get you back again.

III

AGAINST AUTOBIOGRAPHY

Once, the day was this one,
the color of ash and ripening peaches
through the green hair of the willow
sunlight sifting like flour.
There is an instant between breaths
when speech is impossible,
though the lark drools his milky lyric
when no other lark is around.
Then, of course, we say what we mean,
foraging the minutes
sweetened by the weightless blood
of the lettuce, and the ham
that is the color of a little girl's room,
and bread and whatever drink
lightens us. Then we come
again to the same place
between breath, between words,
the mosquitoes horny and our hearts
putting out for anyone, the child's
cheap drunk of holding the breath
and whirling till the face
blackens: often,
at this bottom, this ravine,
I remember water, afternoons
loopy with one window
and the sundusting rays, a thought
that focuses and spits
the gray blood of stump marrow.
The lizard watches from a crevice,
his scaly flame paranoiac
beyond the deepest sull of heifers,
a little blue flume of time,
single driblet of the blood of stone.
My mother is fixing sandwiches.
My father climbs the hill
blistered with water, preening
like a goose in the clay
and pine needles. His breath
comes quickly through the bees
singing their one note flat
song we never learned, flight.
Breathe and breathe again
and think of coming from a star,
of opening in dirt
and closing, the calyx
of the body drawing and releasing
its own cradle. Tell yourself

the wind begins here. Expect
that it will go somewhere.
Say that the lizard was never there,
that it was another lizard,
that it was another day, not
this one, not this wind
the leaves shrugged off.

When the bones came for me
Before I thought *morning, sun,* when it was still a taste,
Oyster and eggwine
That flower of the stomach
Whose roots tapped the dream liquor
Whose stem is a feather in the throat,
I went into my feet, snapping up into the ankles, up
Over the edge of the mattress,
With the spine pressing into the skull,
The hardwood floor cool like marble,
And thought of the man on the train,
For no reason, thought of him telling how once
In a drying out house in Kentucky
A coral snake, blunt and ribboned, came
Spiraling up from his pillow
And he flinched at the quick, lethal
Bite, but already evanescing,
Before my bones were with me
When I was not used to it yet.

My sister used to dollop whole spoons
Of Jell-O into my sleeping palms
So that, waking, I might recognize it,
Between the strangeness of night
And the strangeness of day,
The substance of the eye squeezed to water,
Familiar and melting in the sun.

Now between two worlds the witches have defined,
The one the fingers mistakenly trust, the other
Tunneled between the eyes, dreamed or remembered,
I put on my clothes/shadow fleet in the mirror:
If I see it quick enough and look away
Orange is blue, the amaranth dull
And the forest, not trees, but a print
In a dress my grandmother once wore.
If I look at it long enough, it is the day
As I write it, as the eye looks in
At the eye, as the sun sees us and does not see us.

Here is the poem of noon, the poem of doors.
The word *I* knocks at the word *you*.
No one is home.
And later, when the light comes
Incomprehensibly to the frozen mop on the yard
When each crystal of frost releases its tear,
And I have written it, glazed note
From the torn eye of summer, it remains,
Both unexplained and inexplicable.

When I look up from the desk, it is night.
It is this woman, Virginia, her hand a hummingbird
On my shoulder, her voice
Telling me *eat, eat,* then of her day
Which was not good, which darkens.
And I light the candle, that scent
Which wavers between pig and heaven.
When bone calls to bone, blind as the moon is blind,
Let the day lie down in the night.
I have no opinions now.

BEFORE THE BREAK WITH MARY HOGAN

Before the break with Mary Hogan
I ascended with the only clean hands in the garage
and, atop the greaserack, dreamed
on, came to the future
that was dark, some other place.

Not this one, where silence is a watchdog,
not the last one, neighboring the actual dogs.
The itinerary varies: jobs and arrivals.
Lately my wife has been taking the poor
for picnics in her sleep.

Dear Mary Hogan, what has transpired?
Your big ideas were caulking in the grooves
of 1966. Soon I know
I'll pick up a novel and find your breasts
floating out over the third chapter.

Tell me, has history made us interesting,
or will we always lust, over photographs and gin,
for our former selves as they waited
to be sprung to a future where, not badly, but sure,
no life has gone as planned.

I pass many yellow flowers on the way.
Forgotten. Six bound volumes,
The Flora & Fauna of The Southern Unakas.
With every drink I lose a lake
And feeder rivers, the creeks high on May
Now dryly repeating, stone after stone.

How many cells an ounce, the rate of dying?
What sticks is art. 1937 in the skin
Of a beech, Wilma + James
A palm's width from the one-breasted stick
Woman riding the carved prick to her lover.
What sticks is beggar's lice and black mud.

I drink to the one beech I remember.
It swells beneath my face in the night window.
Remembered water narrows. Power lines hum
Baritone over my head and this creek,
Called Sally Mack, shoals. I can leap it
Easily now and pick up what's thrown ahead—

The sandwiches, still warm, the ice unmelted
In the jars. I think I even kneel,
Drink in mist blown from a fissure in the rock.
I drink from Blowing Spring. I think
Of a saurian locked in limestone, his breath
A cloud of fern, a last meal which has not settled.

And you, who were beside me, are beside me.

You could only offer the body an idea
where a friend's wife had offered herself.

You thought it might help to pretend
you were elsewhere; by that distance,
absolving all loveliness of presence into
the worst sensations from the past:

it is a wound the child has inflicted
on himself, as in penance, for causing pain,
the hideous face the adult must kiss,
and, in kissing, love his own distaste.

Anesthesia, commonest of needs: arms crossed,
eyes fixed, you stared into the horrible.
Was it her hair's reflection on the coffee table?

At one moment you acceded to honor, a pinnacle
where deciding not to, you did anyway.

Later you knew you would have to make wings
excuses; the woman you had married,
who you had always so affectionately wanted
to call "order" would be suspicious.

This affection had only been handled roughly,
the patina cracked. Why worry?

Sandwiches as fresh as the wife's sleep
had been prepared, a can opened quietly.
So your mind went as far away as rodeo,
then turned: how well you recognized that maze.

Until now, these acts had been your planning,
you, your own best audience, seeing as
from a balcony, times when you seemed adrift,
detached from nerves and buoyant over women.

Now, without calculation, was your name
called by your friend, his wife and your own.

You would be the first to say the moral
in this truth: "nothing had happened."

Who would believe you? One crystal at a time
the frost was leaving the beer can
and the moon was the rug on the linoleum.

But as the present is a table where this poem
will return always to acts of recent eminence,
the subject of honor is the friend's wife
as you are aware of her body,

glowing. She has never wanted any thing
more than the sadness conveyed by your touch,
a perversion, like technology, becoming necessary.

So *honor*, the idea you offered the body,
produced by the wife, husband and nation:
had that not required absolute willingness
to sacrifice all pleasure? for the common good?

In fact, weren't you for a moment there
the reluctant virgin,
bathed, perfumed, dressed all in white
and poised, like a sparrow, at the edge?

CRUSHED OBJECTS AT THE BOTTOM OF A STILL POOL

At the end of its usefulness
And the beginning of its present

Shape, it took three men
And a woman who watched and made

Suggestions to cast the unworking
Stove into an upstream pool. But

Rains came for three weeks running
Off the mountainsides, carrying the

Best parts of fields, confetti
Of Styrofoam and mica, bloated

Carcasses, mayonnaise jars and the
Stove, bottled up in narrowing

Boulders, finally with a last shove
From clouds rocked forth into

Rapids and settled in
This deep pool where bream suck

The foodless, battered door.
Almost, we have been cleansed.

EXTENSIONS OF WATTS BAR DAM

Here where bass flip and stagger
to a dazzle of slow blue water
carp dive to alluvium where human

divers won't swim. Locals will say
catfish bigger than men sleep there,
just waiting. But the current is plenty

to keep men in boats; logs, buried
in bottom silt, bloom free, swivel,
then splinter against the wall.

The dam itself is a postcard on which
an official writes by the lights of dials
an afternoon's program for the river.

Through the turbines, the idiom
picks up, becomes the thrumming song,
the giant's voice in chains,

the housewife hears—about how
the water spills everything: obscenities,
threnodies, or no, how the current

catches fires, races through vacuum
cleaners, sewing machines, mixers.
Or it is all in dreaming. The faces

of shoals are locked under a lid
of water and the key has been lost.
Now Oak Ridge burns in the cobalt

distances, and we know no anodyne
to ease that pain
or the beauty of this river

curving in its sheath
like a long blue scimitar
running too deep to return.

What was a mountain is a hill
And what was the top of a hill
Is a valley between the hills
That were mountains. Now that
The world is smaller you may
Take a part of it in your hands
That was hands, knees and skulls,
The dirt cleaned through bread.
On a backbone ridge, or shoreline,
The drive past small baitshops
And trailers toward recreation
Sees only morning or afternoon:
A place the sky might touch
Is a river trapped by valley.
Though that too slipped the pale
Locks of many closed fingers
The thought is for all earth—
Where you lived once—under
The lake where houses are boards
And they wash up all the time
While here the deer have grown
Gills, wings adapted to fins
And moles still trip to rupture
The tender skin of the garden.
Or if it could be seen, far
Below the fisherman who floats
"Above it all," say through
The eyes of lures he lets down,
In the blue of sleet and pines
Someone with an ax would begin
To weave his rooms toward now,
Driftwood silvered in dock light,
A weathering we throw back
To the wrinkled face of the waters—
    Old Hezekiah Hamblen,
Three cabins down the trail.

AQUARIUS

My mother got a neighbor
in her system who would not leave,
a quiet boy who diving
in a quarry pool for stones
went too far. In a moonscape
mossed over, a cold hand
slipped between his ribs
and dialed her number. In dreams
she saw that face becoming
mine, a powdered doll afloat
on funeral wreaths, sinking like a post.
Wherever I went, her voice
put on black clothes and followed,
haunting me back to our yard.
Every night I watched the moon's
yellow scissors draw blood.
Every day I could feel
the sun collect my friends
to shores I only sensed,
water deeper than breath—
I bore it in my hands.
Her face in the window like a sun,
and me on my belly,
cupping that shallow grass, pulling
and pulling: how could I tell
her how difficult that stroke,
how hard to swim in the earth?

IV

It was not that simple, though the marquees
Teased you with knickknacks: *if*
The sight of the naked anatomy offends you
Do not enter. And many turned away

Turned pale, saying "but think for awhile
Of all that is lovely" and they thought
Of cathedrals, of maple leaves in October.
You saw that for those breast would always be

"Unnatural," the Pussycat filled with fiends:
They wanted landscapes and the word magnificent.
You wanted the paradox "wild but controlled,"
To have both sides, the solitude and the friends.

That is why, when much was offered, vegetable
And flesh, you tried one of each, not
Just the cornish hen garnished in sherry
But the sardines, crackers and potted meat,

And you walked into the theatre, shameless
Among those laps covered with newspapers, because
You wanted to see her, to know what it was,
You wanted the camera inside the heart.

THE WHITTLER HUMS AMAZING GRACE

He was proud of camouflage, his hair,
the smoke dissembling over the cabin,
jalopies slipping through the horizon
like smoke. Then it was easy. The mode
of the knife was the mode of the air.

Tuesdays loosened. Cut away the hours,
lay the facts bare. Simpler than that,
he sang as he worked. It wasn't work
really. His daughter swept most into
the fireplace. Crying was not available.

They took his daughter away. Some days,
whittling, whittling, humming and whittling,
he would shave sawdust from the last image,
a horse so small, it bolted through
the crack in the floor. Some days,

the song had no notes. Some days no words.
Some days he neither sang nor whittled.
When the first helicopter passed over,
when the government changed, there was
nothing to stop it. The rain fell down

his chimney. There was nothing to stop
it. His blanket became a tent. Humming
he whittled a wife and bedsheet. Slept,
but one hand still hunted for the soft grain
hidden in the wooden layers of the world.

The Lord to Cousin Leroy appeared

with no props but the air

floating diaphanous
twenty feet outside his bedroom window
as a man soared over in a rocket
who was no more than a ghostly possum
snuffling persimmons glistening with dew.

And the Lord spake,
the moving soft thunder in his voice:

"Goldwater"

"Goldwater"

echoed back.

In the shadow of a pot-bellied stove,
a few gathered and heard the word,
Raymond the paraplegic,
Mrs. Lyle, James the mechanic,
heard the soft rush of gold water
over black bodies
in a sanctuary stinking with Wildroot Creme Oil.

While Leroy's voice filled every empty pew,
lest we be tempted by false prophets
to landslides of faith.

Those words vie edgewise among the drumsticks
Away from men, a statesman with vision,
The crooks and drunks we swallowed
With biscuits and washed down with tea:
Think! they strove till their hearts galled black
To carve the sentences at our Sunday dinner
Only cold lemon supreme stole the thunder, philosophy.
Whose governor mashed into potatoes with a fork?
Our spice is Marx, so sharp it blisters the palate,
Aunt so and so telegraphing her talk
With a scorched wince: "it's all them that's able
That won't work, mostly colored." It feathers
Our napkins, off-browns, off-yellows, and father
Bless him, pontificates: *freedom's pissing off the porch.*

WALKING HOME FROM THE SERMON

When “the way” turned earthly again
it was a gorged knuckle of blue chert
wounding a pasture where sheep
lowed to a sky curdled with solder-
colored, moonstruck stratus,
and heavy behind us as heaven,
the ghost cock of the steeple.
All adults
gone honking ahead, their highest
gears neutral beyond the last audible hill,
I stopped
with Noah Lanningham and Coyd Flowers, Jr.
Jesus, that sky got in our throats.
The boards of the new bridge still quivered,
the creek warped in muddy hackles
beneath the cracks. Late July.
Dog trumpeting and the lemony dribbling
of morning glories, stars like morning
ashes in a hearth: our eyes rose
as though to perfect replicas of bombers.
“But what if gravity wouldn’t work?”
Coyd whispered, and all the ambiguities
from book and dream, from the ponderous
schooling of the muscles, ganged up—
Up I fell, barefooted, through the Milky
Way’s hot taffy, tangled my knot
on the Pleiades, racing by the apostles,
hard on the terrible souls of emperors,
the nether whipping out its honed swords,
its gaggles of goose-tailed meteors
till the least bow-knot of light
bloomed cold as a frog, and out of that deep
height, no God, but Noah’s voice—
“Willard says you just put your thing
in a girl and piss. Babies sprout
up. They grow down there like peas.”
“Aw Noah.”
Coyd spat glibly in the ditch. Around
us stretched a hundred little hills,
pike, moon and pasture, on and on,
keening to the breaking of a single stick.
“But just think, if you was to fall
and nothing to stop it, how far would you go?”

THE MAN WHO COLLECTS EMPTIES

The failure to make distinctions—
between beer and piss or guns
and toys—centers his brain like
a compulsive rider none of us envy.
Oh and how his eyes flare up!
Such illuminations! though quickly
dimmed, sentences shorn at the noun,
anomalies, embarrassing anecdotes.

What has the barber done with his hair?
And his chin, dimpled wrong, biscuit pale.
On that snowy ghost picture in his skull,
he sees the whole town, a trail
of pop bottles, a row of gleaming nickels,
the sleet in wind that suits him fine.

FOR MY FRIEND SHOT SIX TIMES BY AN IRATE HUSBAND

Glenn got shot.
Six times in the half dark
While the sun was locked
In another time zone

The dull bullets
Jammed through his neck
Like tiny kamikazes
And his hair exploded

Like a bag. That was all.
By the time I got
The call it was light.
I sat in the kitchen, musing,

Scorching my hands,
Watching the morning
Open its umbrellas of blood.
When reporters came

Turning the body over and over
Like an invitation
I said nothing.
Dead men don't do

Unearthly things,
Certainly almost never
The remarkable buck and roll
The sexy, epical fidgeting

You see sometimes
In the old westerns.
Death has no sides:
When men die

They die inward
And their knees crackle and pop
Like bad connections.
When Glenn got shot

He fell simply
And heard
In near wiregrass
The last obsidian rustle

Of the splintered wings
Of dead june bugs
The children had left to rot.
Not that it shocked

Us; he drank
Straight whiskey
And drove a truck
But we were distressed

To carry the cumbersome
Baggage of emptiness
Step by step
Through the town's voices

Turning, turned all
The way up on the googol-
Gospeled jukebox of grief
And mental pain. Glenn

I am going to put you down here.
There is nowhere to go.
Souls or systems
We are conveyed by absences

To actions impossible
For others to comprehend.
Now old men stand around
And talk of your going. They nod

Like drugged Shetland ponies.
They are disheartened
As strikebreakers.
They fear you, your settlement,

Or worse: under
The closed roads invisible
Dust trucks are picking
Up the universe.

ORDERS TO THE SECOND SHIFT

I worked there
that summer the war ended
our feelings about it,
learned the properties
of zinc, magnesium, copper,
how much they would take,
what they would return.

A man from time control
who sold those rubbers
they call "french ticklers"
had a word with me one day.
His son was an architect
in Los Angeles.

"These things ain't pipe.
We call them tube."

They went in air conditioners
or were chopped into rings
for the casings of shells.
No one seemed to know.

Only Eric loved the machines
for their pure function
but Eric was stranger than the machines.
He had known Hitler a little
and liked him.

The rest of us listened for Po Po's orders
and the machines were nothing
but bottles of noise, dying
horsepowers, the morning we did not hear
coming out of the tunnel.

ANDREW JACKSON

Nothing so right
as a statue

with nothing
up his sleeve

as if the dead
thought twice which

giants to leave
among the living

held one final
vote deciding

on soldiers
and politicians.

LOOSE ENDS

A terminal uncle, the boy with one arm
forgetting and learning to tie his shoelaces,

or that model who talked a solid hour
and left without mentioning her name:

aren't we uncomfortable with those half
cast memories, the stories of death

never resolved? If those kisses are promises
they've been broken, those lies without charm.

And yet my uncle lies green in his bed,
his one arm the bad dream of the model

sleeping again beside her suitcase of wigs:
each coming to a night so personal

it fails to meet me, loose ends frayed
and fraying, each moment widowed from the other.

V

WEDNESDAY NIGHT

for Everette Maddox

From the one oak in Crestline, darkness is falling
Is driven into the cloned bricks of duplicate houses
Measuring the lawns between the floodlights of the insecure
Until traffic nudges the last laborers gently home
And the late show shrinks to a tiny, azure star
In the living room of the widow on the corner of Elm.
Nightly walking the moon past those houses, I pull down
The brim of my hat with the stealth of a spy or burglar
Knowing that to be caught is to be pinned by the shoulders
While a salesman from Bradley Hardware sinks
Two twenty penny nails in my front teeth, demanding information
About Kupinski, laid out clean on white marble
In Milan, about the disappearance of the Premier's niece,
About the increase in the price of staple-guns
And the deterioration in the quality of plumbing tools.

I walk quietly my intimate crimes, among these lives
That stand to the back like maids in a low budget movie
For whom no shadow lives to lead the way,
Only the drift, like the drift of leaves and shrubbery,
To the most inaccessible shop of the brain,
Where no customer is welcome, and no narrative possible:
There, several children with dirty faces are gathered
Around the supine dwarf, or a ladder of ice
Is raised into unseeable heights of smoke and screams.

Out here, the lesser night stalls in frogs and sludge.
Behind neon arteries of names, the shops are closed.
The only two literate drunks in town have left
The party carrying their drinks in plastic cups.
In the parlor of the funeral home, a family
Begins to regret all former knowledge of the deceased.

What does it come to old friend? In each pore
Of the garden inhaling sweet dew, in each radish extending
A bean's length into the future?

The good man lies down with his wife, the mantra
Of the electric clock hums beside them: thus,
Their faces redden with faint, luminescent digits.
But underneath those faces, mum tissue releases
The dream no images of which will be remembered:
The young who have touched again, finding the skin
Pink and bearable, and their parents aging
Into pillows, who in turn, dream themselves young.

But when I had walked, the town was still there,
And, sober again, I stood away from the sleepers,
Looking into their faces. There was a pressure
Keeping us distant; *that* seemed to implicate everyone,
Only one would not be held back, who sleeps in my bed.
And you out there, who are approaching, from night
To night, this level: lie loose, sleep, trust me
As when once you were the only man awake in this world.

BEAN STATION, LATE TWENTIES: A LETTER TO FRED CHAPPELL

1.

A time comes when all work
that is not finished must
be abandoned, "the best part
of your life!" So falling
on bad times (a wastebasket),
those letters open sad, accusative
eyes, whole days go blank,
the fire goes out of them
as when two cars meet in a downpour
and the lights briefly cross,
dimmed in salutation.

2.

We came here to be alone,
for the best of reasons, escape
from the ordinary
and because no other place
made itself so available,
came to this Victorian trollop
of a house, where not one door
fit its frame perfectly,
and the wind made itself at home,
and the plants got our
attention first, by dying.

3.

To learn how to be here
I went away. A small party
met me with glasses lifted.
It was dawn. They left me
alone with a lovely woman
who read my palm. She said,
"Expect irregularity and insomnia,"
but on the bus home, I slept,
hearing an ex-ringmaster tell
a quiet murderer of parakeets
how the circus got away.

4.

Always one morning, one view,
and it is a vision for cows:
barely a star in the corner
of the eye where desire
and memory cross, a "pee-on-ya"
not peony, if it is Bean Station,
jonquils, not flypoison,
and Delbert McNutt answering
Coy Willett: "No, I was not
born in a barn, but I know
a jackass when I see one."

5.

We learned to be what the place
required without becoming
the place: accent and a distance.
In the daily improvisations
of the flesh, we came to believe
such conversation might go on
for forty years without exhausting
the source of its particulars.
We were taught that by an old
woman, and believing, we were
damned, and deserved each other.

6.

If it is not this way, it should be—
Our grandmothers would have
got along, their skin like birdlegs.
We combed their hair until
it became a long afternoon falling
across the shoulders of farms.
When it became a river, we followed
for rest until it poured into the sea.
When their words were wind again,
we stood at the shore, happy.
We had their eyes.

7.

Remember in your late twenties
morning's insane caroling
of sunlight muddled as dumplings,
when each pebble lacing your
sidewalk was lit from within—
the decision to live always
with one woman and the recognition
that the old, though their voices
ravished the past, represented
the future, a folding-in you
wrote all the way out of itself.

8.

Eloquence
is the deodorant of the intellect.
Words measure the world's right
stench, but prayers on our breath
give us away. At night when
grief makes a black barbell out
of the telephone, far out on
the plateau of rain, on a line
swaybacked as a logging mule
from holding the houses together,
starlings hang on every word.

9.

What was it you were about to say
when the bottle was siphoned
to Coltrane, Ives and Baudelaire,
when heaven was still tropical
and the sun's claw moved slowly over
the cracked dust cover
of the turntable? Morning
turned to morning, the new page
interrupting the old sentence. Today
are you forty? As though a gauge
might monitor life for middle age?

10.

In this cold, what's to get across
since snowdrifts asphyxiate
the traveler, the singer freezes
in the amplifier, and between us
small crafts crash in the mountains?
In such weather, when the self
must entertain itself, both speaker
and listener, from the absolute
punctuation of silence, old friend,
blessing on you: look for the right star,
whistle three perfect notes.

A CURE FOR SHAPES

There is a glaze over
the air. So many zones
we will never touch.

The face in the window
of the passing limousine.
The breath of the majorette

on the billboard.
Sacred for this absence
of hands. For touch

does change the mountain.
And form itself
becomes an occupation.

Although at night
some malevolent union
of intangibles

seems to be at work.
And by morning the self
is picketed with feelings.

I'm willing to admit
my own privacy to your keeping.
You say we shared

that moment equally.
Reading on the commode.
Or a thought at the edge

of a lawn. My notion
of the shape that held me
even as I might enter

her with feeling
becomes a notion of desire.
Or a departure from sense

I might compare to this moment.
Both of us walking out into the night.
The night without stars or objects.

The Story They Told Us of Light

WAS TYPESET USING A

MERGENTHALER 606 IN CALEDONIA

BY AKRA DATA CORP., BIRMINGHAM, ALABAMA.

PRINTING WAS DONE BY THOMSON SHORE, INC.,

OF DEXTER, MICHIGAN, AND THE

BINDER WAS JOHN H. DEKKER AND SONS,

GRAND RAPIDS, MICHIGAN.

BOOK AND JACKET DESIGN: ANNA F. JACOBS

PRODUCTION: PAUL R. KENNEDY